Guia de estudio para el examen de ciudadania estadounidense en Español e Inglés

Mike Swedenberg

Study Guide
100 Questions and Answers for the
US Immigration Test in Spanish and English
Para hacerse ciudadano naturalizado de Estados Unidos, usted debe aprobar
el examen de naturalización, que se hace en la entrevista de naturalización.
Durante la entrevista de naturalización, necesitará contestar preguntas sobre
su Solicitud de Naturalización, Formulario N-400 y sus antecedentes.
También tomará un examen de inglés y educación cívica, a menos que sea
elegible para una exención o una dispensa.Updated 2017

Estudiar estas preguntas no garantiza la obtención
de Ciudadanía a los Estados Unidos

Studying these questions does not guarantee obtaining
citizenship to the United States.

Bi Lingual Languages available:
Spanish, Polish, Chinese, Arabic, Albanian, French, Portuguese, Russian,
Korean, Vietnamese and Tagalog.
In Print and eBooks at Amazon.com

ISBN-13:
978-1514714867

ISBN-10:
1514714868

DEDICACIÓN

Para aquellos que deseen ser ciudadanos estadounidenses

CONTENTS

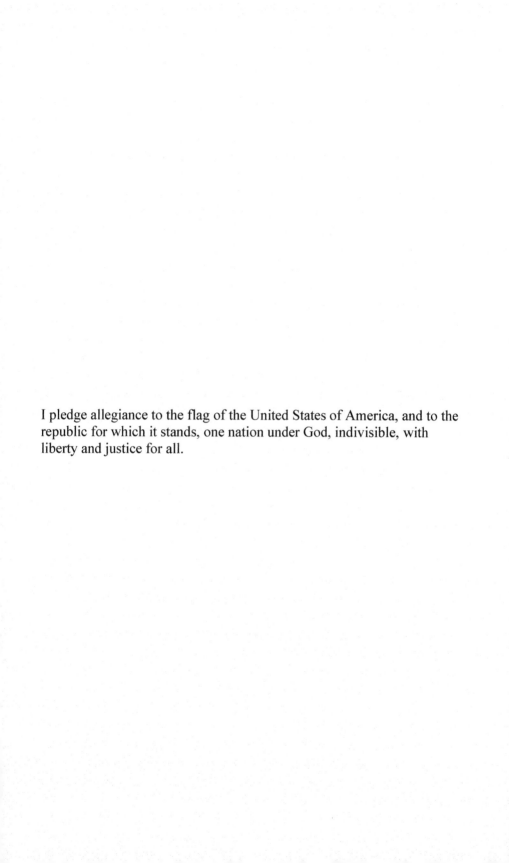

I pledge allegiance to the flag of the United States of America, and to the republic for which it stands, one nation under God, indivisible, with liberty and justice for all.

MUCHAS GRACIAS

US Citizenship and Immigration Service
Edith Delone
Christopher Kurczaba Esq. Chicago Illinois ..

INTRODUCTION

The 100 sample questions and answers for the US Immigration test are listed below. The test is an oral exam in which the USCIS Officer will ask you up to 10 of the 100 questions. You must answer six out of ten questions correctly to pass the civics portion of the test.

On the naturalization test, some answers may change because of elections or appointments. As you study for the test, make sure that you know the most current members of Congress, Senate, Speaker of the House and Governor of your state and district.

This publication is the only study guide that provides this information and updates it throughout the year.

We also provide you with the Sample Written Questions which all applicants must know how to write in English.

INTRODUCCIÓN

Las 100 preguntas de muestra y sus respuestas para la prueba de Inmigración de EEUU, están listadas abajo. La prueba es un examen oral en el que el Oficial de USCIS le preguntará hasta 10 de las 100 preguntas. Usted debe responder seis de diez preguntas correctamente para pasar la parte de civismo de la prueba. En la prueba de nacionalización, algunas respuestas podrían cambiar debido a las elecciones y nombramientos. A medida que usted estudie para la prueba, asegúrese de que usted conoce la mayoría de miembros actuales del congreso, senado, vocero de la cámara y el gobernador de su estado y distrito.

Esta publicación es la única guía de estudio que provee esta información y la actualiza a lo largo del año. También le proveemos con la muestra de preguntas escritas, que todos los aplicantes deben conocer como escribir en Ingles.

Advice from the Immigration Law offices of Christopher Kurczaba

6219 N Milwaukee Ave, Chicago, IL 60646

(773) 774-0011

KurczabaLaw@sbcglobal.net

Three Tests for Citizenship

Most applicants for citizenship or naturalization as it is called, are actually subject to THREE different "tests" when applying. It is important that an individual understand that in applying for Citizenship their entire immigration history is being reviewed and an Immigration Officer is making a determination not only over whether an applicant passes a test, but moreover, is reviewing the applicant's entire immigration history.

The Citizenship process should be looked upon as a complex, detailed demanding process, not just the completion of a form and passing of a simple civics test. This is not a process that should be taken lightly. Often persons get "free" help with benevolent charities completing applications during large scale meetings. However, an applicant can face severe consequences including the loss of their permanent residency and even removal from the United States if certain matters come to the attention of an Immigration Officer reviewing your application.

First and foremost are persons who have ever been arrested, detained or even stopped by a Police Officer. These individuals should ensure they seek the assistance of an attorney to review their criminal record before proceeding with the filing of an application for Citizenship.

Each Applicant for Citizenship undergoes three tests:

1. Test of Civics/History/Government, Reading & Writing

    a. Civics/history test of 10 questions chosen out of a possible 100

b. Reading – applicants will be asked to read out loud a sample sentence from a fixed set of possible sentences

c. Writing – applicants will be asked to write a sentence dictated by an Immigration Officer.

2. Ability to Communicate in English

a. The Immigration Officer will review your application with you. Traditionally, this takes place after you pass your test. This portion can be difficult for those that do not speak English well.

b. The Immigration Officer will speak to you in English to determine if you generally can communicate.

3. Eligibility –a review of an Applicant's personal history

a. The Immigration Officer will review your entire immigration file and determine if you have the proper character to become a citizen. The Officer will literally have before them your entire immigration history including every form and piece of paper that you submitted to the Immigration Service. This includes your applications for immigration benefits before permanent residency.

i. The Officer will review how you obtained your green card or permanent residency.

1. If you received your permanent residency through marriage to a US Citizen, then the Immigration Officer will ask questions about your marriage. The Officer can question whether the marriage was legitimate.

2. If you received your permanent residency through a family member – the Immigration Officer will review your original application to make sure there were no improprieties when you applied.

3. If you received your permanent residency through an employer – the Immigration Officer can ask you questions about the employer and the employment relationship.

ii. The Officer will review your criminal background – checking if you were ever arrested/detained/stopped by a Police Officer at home or abroad.

1. For the Immigration Service- to be stopped, arrested or detained means precisely that – any time a Police agency would take your fingerprints

a. Regardless of the eventual outcome of the case – or what you think it means to be arrested – you will be expected to admit to all times that you were arrested/stopped or detained by a Police agency.

i. Sometimes applicants believe that an arrest means serving time in jail. But the Immigration Service has a much broader interpretation – including anytime that a Police agency would take your fingerprints and record the information.

ii. The Immigration Service obtains criminal background information on individuals primarily from the FBI. The FBI retains this information forever, regardless of expungements, or local agencies clearing of a criminal history.

Asesoría de las oficinas de inmigración de Christopher Kurczaba
6219 N Milwaukee Ave, Chicago, IL 60646
(773) 774-0011
KurczabaLaw@sbcglobal.net

Tres pruebas para la ciudadanía

La mayoría de los aplicantes a la ciudadanía o nacionalización como se les llama, en realidad son sujetos a TRES pruebas cuando están aplicando. Es importante que un individuo entienda que al aplicar para la Ciudadanía su historial completo de inmigración esta siendo revisado y un Oficial de Inmigración no solo está tomando una decisión sobre si el aplicante pasa una prueba, si no que además esta revisando el historial completo de inmigración del aplicante.

El proceso de Ciudadanía debe ser considerado como un proceso complejo, proceso que demanda detalle, no solo el completado de un formulario y pasar una prueba de civismo. Este es un proceso que no debe tomarse a la ligera. A menudo persona reciben ayuda "gratis" de caridades benevolentes para completar las solicitudes en reuniones a gran escala. Sin embargo, un aplicante puede enfrentar severas consecuencias incluyendo la perdida de su residencia permanente incluso la deportación de los Estados Unidos si ciertas cosas llaman la atención del Oficial de Inmigración que revisa su solicitud. Primero y ante todo personas que alguna vez han sido arrestadas, detenidas o paradas por un Oficial de la Policía. Estos individuos deben asegurarse de buscar asistencia de un abogado para revisar su récord criminal antes de proceder con el llenado de la solicitud de Ciudadanía.

Cada uno de los aplicantes a Ciudadanía se someten a tres pruebas:

1. Prueba de Civismo/Historia/Gobierno, Lectura y Escritura
   a) Prueba de 10 preguntas sobre civismo/historia, elegidas de 100 preguntas posibles.
   b) Lectura: Se le pedirá al solicitante leer en voz alta una oración de muestra de un conjunto de oraciones posibles.
   c) Escritura: Se le pedirá al aplicante que escriba una oración dictada por un Oficial de inmigración.
2. Habilidad para comunicarse en Ingles
   a) El oficial de inmigración revisará su aplicación con usted. Tradicionalmente, esto toma lugar después de que usted pasa su prueba. Esta parte puede ser difícil para aquellos que no hablan bien el ingles.
   b) El Oficial de Inmigración le hablará en Ingles para determinar si usted puede comunicarse generalmente.
3. Elegibilidad: la revisión del historial personal de un aplicante
   a) El Oficial de Inmigración revisará su archivo de inmigración entero y para determinar si usted tiene el carácter adecuado para convertirse en un ciudadano. El Oficial tendrá literalmente enfrente su historial completo de inmigración incluyendo cada formulario y pedazo de papel que usted envió al Servicio de Inmigración. Esto incluye sus solicitudes para beneficios de inmigración antes de la residencia permanente.

i. El oficial revisará como obtuvo su "green card" o su residencia permanente.

1. Si usted recibe su residencia permanente a través de casarse con un ciudadano de Estados Unidos, entonces el Oficial de

Inmigración le preguntará sobre su matrimonio. El Oficial puede preguntar si su matrimonio es legítimo.

2. Si usted recibe su residencia permanente a través de un miembro de la familia, el Oficial de Inmigración revisará su solicitud original para asegurarse de que no hubieron inconvenientes cuando aplicó.

3. Si usted recibe su residencia permanente a través de un empleador, el Oficial de Inmigración puede preguntarle sobre el empleador y la relación de empleo.

ii. El Oficial revisará sus antecedentes penales: verificando si usted fue arrestado/detenido/parado por un Oficial de la Policía en el país o en el extranjero.

1. Para el servicio de Inmigración- ser parado, arrestado o detenido significa precisamente eso, cada vez que una agencia de Policía toma sus huellas dactilares.

   a) Independientemente del resultado final del caso,o lo que usted piensa que significa ser arrestado/parado o detenido por una agencia de policía.

   i. A veces los aplicantes piensan que un arresto significa tiempo de servicio en prisión. Pero el Servicio de Inmigración tiene una interpretación más amplia, incluyendo cualquier momento que una agencia de Policía haya tomado sus huellas dactilares y registrado la información.

El Servicio de Inmigración obtiene la información antecedentes penales de los individuos, principalmente del FBI. El FBI retiene esta información para siempre, independientemente sin han sido borrados, o si el historial criminal ha sido limpiado por agencias locales

TRANSLATOR INTRODUCTION

Hello, my name is Edith DeLeon. I was born in Quito, Ecuador. My parents are Ecuadorians and I'm very proud to be Ecuadorian-American.

I grew up with both cultures. I had the opportunity to study at a college and become a citizen of the United States. I have prospered and I own my home and business in New York and North Carolina. I also work for a company of Certified Public Accountants in the department of information technology for 23 years.

I have a beautiful family, husband and 2 daughters, who also reap the benefits of being born and growing up in the U.S.

One problem with the citizenship test is access to the questions and answers to study. Professor Domiciliary makes this task easier and inexpensive. The professor asked me to help create this new study guide just for you.

Now you have a sample of the questions in Spanish and English.

Thank you very much.
Edith

Hola, mi nombre es Edith DeLeon- nací en Quito, Ecuador. Mis padres son Ecuatorianos.

Yo estoy muy orgullosa de ser Ecuatoriana-Americana, crecí con las dos culturas. Tuve la oportunidad de estudiar en un Colegio y hacerme una ciudadana própera de los E.U.Actualmente vivo y soy propietaria de mi casa y negocios en New York y North Carolina. Tambien trabajo en una Companía de Contadores, en el departamento de tecnologia e información por 23 años.

Tengo una hermosa familia, esposo y 2 hijas, quienes tambien cosechan los beneficios de nacer y crecer en los E.U.

Uno de los problemas es cogar la prueba de la ciudadania,y tener acceso a las preguntas y respuestas para estudiar. El profesor Domiciliario,hace esta tarea mas facil y muy económica. El Profesor me pidió ayuda para crear este nuevo guía de estudio justo para Usted.

Ahora Ud tiene una muestra de las preguntas en Espanól e Ingles.

Muchas Gracias
Edith

AMERICAN GOVERNMENT

GOBIERNO AMERICANO

I. Principles of American Democracy / Principios de democracia americana

1. What is the supreme law of the land?

> The Constitution

>> ¿Cuál es la legislación nacional suprema?

>> La constitución

2. What does the Constitution do?

> Sets up the government

> Defines the government

> Protects basic rights of Americans

>> ¿Qué hace la constitución?

>> Establece el gobierno

>> Define un gobierno

>> Protege derechos fundamentales de americanos

3. The idea of self-government is in the first three words of the Constitution. What are these words?

> We the People

>> La idea del gobierno autónomo está en las primeras tres palabras de la constitución. ¿Cuáles son estas palabras?

>> Nosotros la gente

7

4. What is an amendment?

A change to the Constitution.

An addition to the Constitution.

¿Cuál es una enmienda?

un cambio a la constitución.

una adición a la constitución.

5. What do we call the first ten amendments to the Constitution?

The Bill of Rights

¿Qué llamamos las primeras diez enmiendas a la constitución?

La Declaración de Derechos

6. What is one right or freedom from the First Amendment? (You need to know one answer)

Speech

Religion

Assembly

Press

Petition the government

¿Cuál es un derecho o libertad de la Primera Enmienda? *(Hay tres respuestas correctas, necesita saber uno)

Discurso

Religion

Asamblea

Guia de estudio

Prensa

Peticion al gobierno

7. How many amendments does the Constitution have?

Twenty-seven (27)

¿Cuántas enmiendas la constitución tiene?

Veintisiete (27)

8. What did the Declaration of Independence do?

Announced our independence (from Great Britain)

Declared our independence (from Great Britain)

Said that the United States is free (from Great Britain)

¿Qué hizo la Declaración de Independencia?

Anunció nuestra independencia (de Gran Bretaña)

Declaró nuestra independencia (de Gran Bretaña)

Declaro que los Estados Unidos están libres (de Gran Bretaña)

9. What are two rights in the Declaration of Independence?

Life

Liberty

Pursuit of Happiness

¿Cuáles son dos derechos en la Declaración de Independencia?

Vida

Libertad

Búsqueda de la felicidad

10. What is freedom of religion?

You can practice any religion, or not practice a religion.

¿Cuál es la libertad de religión?

Puedes practicar cualquier religión, o no practicar una religión.

11. What is the economic system in the United States?*

capitalist economy

market economy

¿Cuál es el sistema económico en los Estados Unidos? *

economía capitalista

economía de mercado

12. What is the "rule of law"?

Everyone must follow the law

Leaders must obey the law.

Government must obey the law.

No one is above the law

Cuáles son las " ¿reglas de las leyes "?

Cada uno debe seguir la ley.

Los líderes deben obedecer la ley.

El gobierno debe obedecer la ley.

Nadie está sobre la ley.

System of Government / Sistema de gobierno

13. Name one branch or part of the government.*

Congress

Legislative

President

Executive

The courts

Judicial

Nombre una rama o porción del govierno.*

Congreso

Legislativo

Presidente

Ejecutivo

Las cortes

Judicial

14. What stops one branch of government from becoming too powerful?

Checks and balances

Separation of powers

> Qué le detine a una rama de gobierno para llegar hacer demasiado poderoso?

> Controles y equilibrios

> Separación de poderes

15. Who is in charge of the executive branch?

The President

> ¿Quién está a cargo del Poder Ejecutivo?

> el presidente

16. Who makes federal laws?

Congress

Senate and House (of Representatives)

(U.S. or national) legislature

> ¿Quién hace las leyes federales?

> Congreso

> Senado (de representantes)

> (los E.E.U.U. o nacional) legislatura

17. What are the two parts of the U.S. Congress?*

The Senate and House (of Representatives)

¿Cuáles son las dos partes del congreso de los E.E.U.U.? *

el Senado y la casa de representantes

18. How many U.S. Senators are there?

One hundred (100)

¿Cuántos senadores de los E.E.U.U. hay?

Cien (100)

19. We elect a U.S. Senator for how many years?

Six (6)

¿Elegimos a senador de los E.E.U.U. por cuántos años?

Seis (6)

20. Who is one of your state's U.S. Senators?*

See Page 39 Write answer here_____

* If you are 65 years old or older and have been a legal permanent resident of the United States for 20 or more years, you may study just the questions that have been marked with an asterisk.

* Si eres 65 años o más y has sido un residente permanente legal de los Estados Unidos por 20 o más años, puedes estudiar apenas las preguntas que se han marcado con un asterisco.

21. The House of Representatives has how many voting members?

Four hundred thirty-five (435)

¿Cuantos miembros votantes tiene La cámara de representantes?

Cuatrocientos treinta y cinco (435)

22. We elect a U.S. Representative for how many years?

Two (2)

¿Elegimos un representante de los E.E.U.U. por cuántos años?

Dos (2)

23. Name your U.S. Representative.

See Page 42 Write answer here_____

24. Who does a U.S. Senator represent?

All people of the state

¿Quién representa un senador de los E.E.U.U.?

Toda la gente del estado

25. Why do some states have more Representatives than other states?

There are three correct answers. You need to know one answer.

Because of the state's population

Because they have more people

Because some states have more people

¿Por qué algunos estados tienen más representantes que otros estados?

Hay tres respuestas correctas, necesita saber uno.

Debido a la población del estado

Porque tienen más gente

Porque algunos estados tienen más gente

26. We elect a President for how many years?

Four (4)

¿Elegimos a presidente por cuántos años?

Cuatro (4)

27. In what month do we vote for President?*

November

¿En qué mes votamos por un presidente? *

Noviembre

28. What is the name of the President of the United States now?*

Barack H. Obama

¿Cuál es el nombre del Presidente de los Estados Unidos ahora? *

Barack H. Obama

29. What is the name of the Vice President of the United States now?

Joseph R. Biden, Jr.

¿Cuál es el nombre del vice presidente de los Estados Unidos ahora?

Joseph R. Biden, Jr.

30. If the President can no longer serve, who becomes President?

The Vice President

¿Si el presidente no puede servir más, quien hace de presidente?

El vice presidente

31. If both the President and the Vice President can no longer serve, who becomes President?

The Speaker of the House

¿Si el presidente y el vice presidente no pueden servir más, quien hace de presidente?

El orador de la casa

32. Who is the Commander in Chief of the military?

The President

¿Quién es el comandante y jefe de los militares?

El presidente

33. Who signs bills to become laws?

The President

¿Quién firma propuestas para convertirse en leyes?

El presidente

34. Who vetoes bills?

   The President

   ¿Quién veta propuestas?

   El presidente

35. What does the President's Cabinet do?

   Advises the President

   ¿Qué hace el Gabinete del presidente?

   Aconseja al presidente

36. What are two Cabinet-level positions?

   Secretary of State

   Secretary of Labor

   Cuáles son dos niveles de posiciones del Cabinete?

   El secretario(a) de Estado

   El secretario(a) del trabajo

37. What does the judicial branch do?

   Reviews laws

   Explains laws

   Resolves disputes (disagreements)

decides if a law goes against the Constitution

¿Que hace la rama judicial?

Revisar leyes

Explica leyes

Resulven los desacuerdos

Decide si una ley va contra la constitución

38. What is the highest court in the United States?

The Supreme Court

¿Cuál es el tribunal más superior de los Estados Unidos?

El Tribunal Supremo

39. How many justices are on the Supreme Court?

Nine (9)

¿Cuántos jueces hay en el Tribunal Supremo?

Nueve (9)

40. Who is the Chief Justice of the United States?

John G. Roberts, Jr.

¿Quién es el principal jues de los Estados Unidos?

John G. Roberts, Jr.

41. Under our Constitution, some powers belong to the federal government. What is one power of the federal government?

Know one of the following:

To print money

To declare war

To create an army

To make treaties

> Bajo nuestra constitución, algunos poderes pertenecen al gobierno federal. ¿Cuál es un poder del gobierno federal?

> Conozca una de las siguientes repuestas:

> Pra imprimir el dinero

> Para declarar guerra

> Para crear a un ejército

> Para hacer trados

42. Under our Constitution, some powers belong to the states. What is one power of the states?

> Provide schooling and education

> Bajo nuestra constitución, algunos poderes pertenecen a los estados. ¿Cuál es un poder de los estados?

> Proporcionar suficiente educación

43. Who is the Governor of your state?

See Page 81 Write answer here_____

44. What is the capital of your state?*

Qual é a capital do seu estado?

See Page: 84 **Write answer here**_____

45. What are the two major political parties in the United States?*

Democratic and Republican

¿Cuáles son los dos partidos políticos principales en los Estados Unidos? *

Demócratas y Republicanos

46. What is the political party of the President now?

Democratic Party

¿Cuál es el partido político del presidente hoy?

Partido Demócratas

47. What is the name of the Speaker of the House of Representatives now?

Paul Ryan

¿Cuál es el nombre del Orador de la Cámara de Representantes hoy?

Paul Ryan

Rights and Responsibilities
Los derechos y responsabilidades

48. There are four amendments to the Constitution about who can vote. Describe one of them.

Citizens eighteen (18) and older can vote.

Any citizen can vote. (Women and men can vote.)

Hay cuatro enmiendas a la constitución sobre quién puede votar. Describa una de ellas.

Ciudadanos de 18 años o mas puede votar.

Cualquier ciudadano puede votar. (Las mujeres y los hombres pueden votar.)

49. What is one responsibility that is only for United States citizens?*

Serve on a jury

¿Cuál es una responsabilidad que tiene un ciudadano de los Estados Unidos? *

Servir en un jurado

50. What are two rights only for United States citizens?

Apply for a federal job

vote

¿Cuáles son los derechos solamente para los ciudadanos de Estados Unidos?

Solicitar un trabajo federal

Votar

51. What are two rights of everyone living in the United States?

Freedom of expression

Freedom of speech

¿Cuáles son los derechos de cada uno que vive en los Estados Unidos?

Libertad de expresión

Libertad de hablar

52. What do we show loyalty to when we say the Pledge of Allegiance?

The United States and the flag

¿A Qué demostramos lealtad cuando hacemos la jura de la bandera?

A los Estados Unidos y la bandera

53. What is one promise you make when you become a United States citizen?

Defend the Constitution and laws of the United States

¿Cuál es la promesa que haces cuando tú te haces un ciudadano de Estados Unidos?

Defender la constitución y las leyes de los Estados Unidos

54. How old do citizens have to be to vote?*

Eighteen (18) and older

¿ Cual es la edad de un ciudadano para votar? *

Dieciocho (18) años y más

55. What are two ways that Americans can participate in their democracy?

Vote

Join a political party

¿Cuáles son dos maneras que los americanos pueden participar en su democracia?

Votar

Ensamblar un partido político

56. When is the last day you can send in federal income tax forms?*

April 15

¿Cuándo es el ultimo día que tú puedes enviar las formulas de impuesto federal? *

15 de abril

57. When must all men register for the Selective Service?

Between eighteen (18) and twenty-six (26)

¿Cuándo deben registrarse todos los hombres para el servicio selectivo?

Entre dieciocho (18) y veintiséis (26) años

AMERICAN HISTORY / HISTORIA AMERICANA
A: Colonial Period and Independence / Período e independencia coloniales

58. What is one reason colonists came to America?

Freedom

Political liberty

¿ Cuál es una razón que los colonizadores vinieron a América?

Libertad

Libertad política

59. Who lived in America before the Europeans arrived?

Native Americans

American Indians

¿Quién vivió en América antes de que llegaran los europeos?

Nativos americanos

Indios americanos

60. What group of people was taken to America and sold as slaves?

Africans

¿ Qué grupo de personas les vendieron en America como esclavos?

Africanos

61. Why did the colonists fight the British?

Because of high taxes (taxation without representation)

Because the British army stayed in their houses (boarding, quartering)

Because they didn't have self-government

¿Por qué los colonizadores lucharon con los Británicos?

Debido a los altos impuestos (impuestos sin la representación)

Porque el ejército británico permanecía en sus casas (en guardia)

Porque no tenían gobierno autónomo

62. Who wrote the Declaration of Independence?

Thomas Jefferson

¿Quién escribió la Declaración de Independencia?

Thomas Jefferson

63. When was the Declaration of Independence adopted?

July 4, 1776

Cuándo fue adoptada la Declaración de Independencia?

De julio de 1776

64. There were 13 original states. Name three.

New York

New Jersey

Virgina

Había 13 estados originales. Nombre tres.

Nueva York

Nueva Jersey

Virginia

65. What happened at the Constitutional Convention?

The Constitution was written.

¿Qué sucedió en la convención constitucional?

La constitución fue escrita.

66. When was the Constitution written?

1787

¿Cuándo fue escrita la constitución?

1787

67. The Federalist Papers supported the passage of the U.S. Constitution. Name one of the writers.

James Madison

Los papeles federalistas apoyaron el paso de la constitución de los E.E.U.U. Nombre uno de los escritores.

James Madison

68. What is one thing Benjamin Franklin is famous for?

U.S. diplomat

¿Por que fue famoso Benjamin Franklin?

Fue diplomatico de los E.E.U.U.

69. Who is the "Father of Our Country"?

George Washington

Quién es el "¿Padre de nuestro pais"?

George Washington

70. Who was the first President?*

George Washington

¿Quién fue el primer presidente? *

George Washington

71. What territory did the United States buy from France in 1803?

The Louisiana Territory

¿Qué territorio los Estados Unidos compro a Francia en 1803?

El territorio de Luisiana

72. Name one war fought by the United States in the 1800s.

Spanish-American War

Nombre una guerra que los Estados Unidos combatió en los años 1800s.

Guerra hispanoamericana

73. Name the U.S. war between the North and the South.

The Civil War

Nombre la guerra de los E.E.U.U. entre el norte y el sur.

La guerra civil

74. Name one problem that led to the Civil War.

Slavery

Nombre un problema que llevó a la guerra civil.

Esclavitud

75. What was one important thing that Abraham Lincoln did?*

Freed the slaves (Emancipation Proclamation)

¿Que cosa importante hizo Abraham Lincoln? *

Liberó los esclavos (la proclamación de la emancipación)

76. What did the Emancipation Proclamation do?

Freed the slaves

¿Qué hizo la proclamación de la emancipación?

Liberó los esclavos

77. What did Susan B. Anthony do?

Fought for women's rights

¿Qué hizo Susan B. Anthony?

Luchó por los derechos de las mujeres

C: Recent American History and Other Important Historical Information

C: La reciente historia americana y otra importante información histórica

78. Name one war fought by the United States in the 1900s.*

World War II

Nombre una guerra de los Estados Unidos en los años 1900s.*

Segunda Guerra Mundial

79. Who was President during World War I?

Woodrow Wilson

¿Quién fue presidente durante la Primera Guerra Mundial?

Woodrow Wilson

80. Who was President during the Great Depression and World War II?

Franklin Roosevelt

¿Quién fue presidente durante la Gran Depresión y la Segunda Guerra Mundial?

Franklin Roosevelt

81. Who did the United States fight in World War II?

Japan, Germany and Italy

¿Con quien peleo los Estados Unidos en la Segunda Guerra Mundial?

Japón, Alemania e Italia

82. Before he was President, Eisenhower was a general. What war was he in?

World War II

Antes que fuera presidente, Eisenhower era un general. ¿En qué guerra estubo él?

Segunda Guerra Mundial

83. During the Cold War, what was the main concern of the United States?

Communism

¿Durante la guerra fría, cuál era la mayor preocupación de los Estados Unidos?

Comunismo

84. What movement tried to end racial discrimination?

civil rights movement

¿Qué movimiento intentó terminar la discriminación racial?

Los derechos civiles (movimiento)

85. What did Martin Luther King, Jr. do?*

Fought for civil rights

¿Qué hizo Martin Luther King, Jr.? *

Luchó por los derechos civiles

86. What major event happened on September 11, 2001 in the United States?

Terrorists attacked the United States.

¿Qué gran evento sucedió el 11 de septiembre de 2001 en los Estados Unidos?

Los terroristas atacaron los Estados Unidos.

87. Name one American Indian tribe in the United States.

Cherokee

Navajo

Apache

Nombre una tribu india americana en los Estados Unidos.

Cherokee

Navajo

Apache

[Adjudicators will be supplied with a complete list.][Suministrarán una lista completa.]

INTEGRATED CIVICS / CíVICO INTEGRADO

Geography /.Geografía

88. Name one of the two longest rivers in the United States.

Missouri or Mississippi river

Nombre uno de los dos ríos más largos en los Estados Unidos.

Rio Missouri o Mississippi

89. What ocean is on the West Coast of the United States?

Pacific Ocean

¿Qué océano está en la costa oeste de los Estados Unidos?

Pacífico

90. What ocean is on the East Coast of the United States?

Atlantic Ocean

¿Qué océano está en la costa este de los Estados Unidos?

Atlántico (océano)

91. Name one U.S. territory.

Puerto Rico

Nombre un territorio de los E.E.U.U..

Puerto Rico

92. Name one state that borders Canada.

New York

Nombre un estado fronterizo con Canadá.

Nueva York

93. Name one state that borders Mexico.

California

Nombre un estado fronterizo con México

California

94. What is the capital of the United States?*

Washington, D.C.

¿Cual ciudad es la capital de los Estados Unidos? *

Washington, D.C.

95. Where is the Statue of Liberty?*

New York Harbor

¿Dónde está la estatua de la libertad? *

En el puerto de Nueva York

Symbols ./. Símbolos

96. Why does the flag have 13 stripes?

Because there were 13 original colonies

¿Por qué la bandera tiene 13 rayas?

Porque había 13 colonias originales

97. Why does the flag have 50 stars?*

Because there is one star for each state

¿Por qué la bandera tiene 50 estrellas? *

Porque hay una estrella por cada estado

98. What is the name of the national anthem?

The Star-Spangled Banner

¿Cuál es el nombre del himno nacional?

The Star-Spangled Banner

Holidays./.Días de fiesta

99. When do we celebrate Independence Day?*

July 4

¿Cuándo celebramos Día de la Independencia? *

4 de Julio

100. Name two national U.S. holidays.

Independence Day

Christmas

Nombre dos días de fiesta nacionales de los E.E.U.U.

Día de la independencia

La Navidad

Sample Written Sentences

You will be asked to write a sample sentence. Normally you can make up to three (3) errors in writing and still pass the test.

Be careful to listen to each word the examiner reads. Make sure to write each word, even if you think it is not needed grammatically, if the examiner reads a word; please write out every word that is dictated.

Muestra Escrita Sentencias

Se le pedirá que escriba una oración de muestra. Normalmente usted puede tener hasta tres (3) errores al escribir y aún pasar la prueba. Sea cuidadoso al escuchar cada palabra que el examinador lee. Asegúrese de escribir cada palabra, incluso si usted piensa que no es necesaria gramáticamente, si el examinador lee una palabra; por favor escriba cada palabra que es dictada.

SAMPLE WRITTEN SENTENCES

You will be asked to write a sample sentence. Normally you can make up to three (3) errors in writing and still pass the test.

Be careful to listen to each word the examiner reads. Make sure to write each word, even if you think it is not needed grammatically, if the examiner reads a word; please write out every word that is dictated.

1) A senator is elected for 6 years.

2) Joseph Biden is the Vice President of the United States.

3) All people want to be free.

4) America is the land of freedom.

5) All American citizens have the right to vote.

6) America is the home of the brave.

7) America is the land of the free.

8) Donald J Trump is the President of the United States.

9) Citizens have the right to vote.

10) Congress is part of the American government.

11) Congress meets in Washington DC.

12) Congress passes laws in the United States.

13) George Washington was the first president.

14) I want to be a citizen of the United States.

15) I want to be an American citizen.

16) I want to become an American so I can vote.

17) It is important for all citizens to vote.

18) Many people come to America for freedom.

19) Many people have died for freedom.

20) Martha Washington was the first lady.

21) Only Congress can declare war.

22) Our Government is divided into three branches.

23) People in America have the right to freedom.

24) People vote for the President in November.

25) The American flag has stars and stripes.

26) The American flag has 13 stripes.

27) The capital of the United States is Washington DC.

28) The colors of the flag are red white and blue.

29) The Constitution is the supreme law of our land.

30) The flag of the United States has 50 stars.

31) The House and Senate are parts of Congress

32) The President enforces the laws.

33) The President has the power of veto.

34) The President is elected every 4 years.

35) The President lives in the White House.

36) The President lives in Washington D.C.

37) The President must be an American citizen.

38) The President must be born in the United States.

39) The President signs bills into law.

40) The stars of the American flag are white.

41) The White House is in Washington, DC.

42) The United States flag is red white and blue.

43) The United States of America has 50 states.

Members of the Senate

Senators of the 114th Congress

Representatives are subject to change.

Find your state to identify your two Senators

Source: http://Senate.gov Updated January 2017

*Newly elected 2016 Subject to change upon Certification

See list below. Answers will vary. For District of Columbia residents and residents of U.S. territories, the answer is that D.C. (or the territory where the applicant lives) has no U.S. Senators.

Alaska: Murkowski, Lisa - (R - AK)   Sullivan, Daniel - (R - AK)

Alabama: Sessions, Jeff - (R - AL)   Shelby, Richard C. - (R - AL)

Arkansas: Boozman, John - (R - AR)   Cotton, Tom - (R - AR)

Arizona: Flake, Jeff - (R - AZ)   McCain, John - (R - AZ)

California: Harris, Kamala- (D - CA)*   Feinstein, Dianne - (D - CA)

Colorado: Bennet, Michael F. - (D - CO)   Gardner, Cory - (R - CO)

Connecticut: Blumenthal, Richard - (D - CT)   Murphy, Christopher - (D - CT)

Delaware: Carper, Thomas R. - (D - DE)   Coons, Christopher A. - (D - DE)

Florida: Nelson, Bill - (D - FL)   Rubio, Marco - (R - FL)

Georgia: Isakson, Johnny - (R - GA)   Perdue, David - (R - GA)

Hawaii: Hirono, Mazie K. - (D - HI)   Schatz, Brian - (D - HI)

Iowa: Ernst, Joni - (R - IA)   Grassley, Chuck - (R - IA)

Idaho: Crapo, Mike - (R - ID)   Risch, James E. - (R - ID)

Illinois: Durbin, Richard J. - (D - IL)   Duckworth, Tammy- (D - IL)*

Indiana: Young, Todd - (R - IN)*   Donnelly, Joe - (D - IN)

Kansas: Moran, Jerry - (R - KS)   Roberts, Pat - (R - KS)

Kentucky: McConnell, Mitch - (R - KY)   Paul, Rand - (R - KY)

Louisiana: Cassidy, Bill - (R - LA)   Kennedy, John - (R - LA)

Massachusetts: Markey, Edward J. - (D - MA)   Warren, Elizabeth - (D - MA)

Maryland: Cardin, Benjamin L. - (D - MD)   Van Hollen, Chris - (D - MD)*

Maine: Collins, Susan M. - (R - ME)   King, Angus S., Jr. - (I - ME)

Michigan: Peters, Gary - (D - MI)   Stabenow, Debbie - (D - MI)

Minnesota: Franken, Al - (D - MN)   Klobuchar, Amy - (D - MN)

Missouri: Blunt, Roy - (R - MO)   McCaskill, Claire - (D - MO)

Mississippi: Cochran, Thad - (R - MS)   Wicker, Roger F. - (R - MS)

Montana: Tester, Jon - (D - MT)   Daines, Steve - (R - MT)

North Carolina: Burr, Richard - (R - NC)   Tillis, Thom - (R - NC)

North Dakota: Heitkamp, Heidi - (D - ND)   Hoeven, John - (R - ND)

Nebraska: Fischer, Deb - (R - NE)   Sasse, Ben - (R - NE)

New Hampshire: Hassan, Maggie- (D - NH)*   Shaheen, Jeanne - (D - NH)

New Jersey: Booker, Cory A. - (D - NJ)   Menendez, Robert - (D - NJ)

New Mexico: Heinrich, Martin - (D - NM)   Udall, Tom - (D - NM)

Nevada: Heller, Dean - (R - NV)   Masto, Catherine Cortez - (D - NV) *

New York: Gillibrand, Kirsten E. - (D - NY)   Schumer, Charles E. - (D - NY)

Ohio: Brown, Sherrod - (D - OH)   Portman, Rob - (R - OH)

Oklahoma: Inhofe, James M. - (R - OK)   Lankford, James - (R - OK)

Oregon: Merkley, Jeff - (D - OR)   Wyden, Ron - (D - OR)

Pennsylvania: Casey, Robert P., Jr. - (D - PA)   Toomey, Patrick J. - (R - PA)

Rhode Island: Reed, Jack - (D - RI)   Whitehouse, Sheldon - (D - RI)

South Carolina: Graham, Lindsey - (R - SC)   Scott, Tim - (R - SC)

South Carolina: Rounds, Mike - (R - SD)   Thune, John - (R - SD)

Tennessee: Alexander, Lamar - (R - TN)   Corker, Bob - (R - TN)

Texas: Cornyn, John - (R - TX)   Cruz, Ted - (R - TX)

Utah: Hatch, Orrin G. - (R - UT)   Lee, Mike - (R - UT)

Virginia: Kaine, Tim - (D - VA)   Warner, Mark R. - (D - VA)

Vermont: Leahy, Patrick J. - (D - VT)   Sanders, Bernard - (I - VT)

Washington: Cantwell, Maria - (D - WA)   Murray, Patty - (D - WA)

Wisconsin: Baldwin, Tammy - (D - WI)   Johnson, Ron - (R - WI)

West Virginia: Capito, Shelley Moore - (R - WV)   Manchin, Joe, III - (D - WV)

Wyoming: Barrasso, John - (R - WY)   Enzi, Michael B. - (R - WY)

Members of the 114th Congress

Find your state and your District Number to identify your Congressperson. You must determine what district you live in to identify your Representative.

Updated January 2017

Source: http://www.house.gov/representatives/

*Newly elected 2016 Subject to change upon Certification
Source:
https://en.wikipedia.org/wiki/United_States_House_of_Representatives_elections,_2016

Alabama

District	Name	Party
1	Byrne, Bradley	R
2	Roby, Martha	R
3	Rogers, Mike	R
4	Aderholt, Robert	R
5	Brooks, Mo	R
6	Palmer, Gary	R
7	Sewell, Terri A.	D

Alaska

District	Name	Party

District	Name	Party
At Large	Young, Don	R

American Samoa

District	Name	Party
At Large	Radewagen, Amata	R

Arizona

District	Name	Party
1	Kirkpatrick, Ann	D
2	McSally, Martha	R
3	Grijalva, Raul	D
4	Gosar, Paul A.	R
5	Salmon, Matt	R
6	Schweikert, David	R
7	Gallego, Ruben	D
8	Franks, Trent	R

District	Name	Party
9	Sinema, Kyrsten	D

Arkansas

District	Name	Party
1	Crawford, Rick	R
2	Hill, French	R
3	Womack, Steve	R
4	Westerman, Bruce	R

California

District	Name	Party
1	LaMalfa, Doug	R
2	Huffman, Jared	D
3	Garamendi, John	D
4	McClintock, Tom	R
5	Thompson, Mike	D

District	Name	Party
6	Matsui, Doris O.	D
7	Bera, Ami	D
8	Cook, Paul	R
9	McNerney, Jerry	D
10	Denham, Jeff	R
11	DeSaulnier, Mark	D
12	Pelosi, Nancy	D
13	Lee, Barbara	D
14	Speier, Jackie	D
15	Swalwell, Eric	D
16	Costa, Jim	D
17	Khanna, Ro *	D
18	Eshoo, Anna G.	D
19	Lofgren, Zoe	D

District	Name	Party
20	Farr, Sam	D
21	Valadao, David	R
22	Nunes, Devin	R
23	McCarthy, Kevin	R
24	Capps, Lois	D
25	Knight, Steve	R
26	Brownley, Julia	D
27	Chu, Judy	D
28	Schiff, Adam	D
29	Cárdenas, Tony	D
30	Sherman, Brad	D
31	Aguilar, Pete	D
32	Napolitano, Grace	D
33	Lieu, Ted	D

District	Name	Party
34	Becerra, Xavier	D
35	Torres, Norma	D
36	Ruiz, Raul	D
37	Bass, Karen	D
38	Sánchez, Linda	D
39	Royce, Ed	R
40	Roybal-Allard, Lucille	D
41	Takano, Mark	D
42	Calvert, Ken	R
43	Waters, Maxine	D
44	Hahn, Janice	D
45	Walters, Mimi	R
46	Sanchez, Loretta	D
47	Lowenthal, Alan	D

District	Name	Party
48	Rohrabacher, Dana	R
49	Issa, Darrell	R
50	Hunter, Duncan D.	R
51	Vargas, Juan	D
52	Peters, Scott	D
53	Davis, Susan	D

Colorado

District	Name	Party
1	DeGette, Diana	D
2	Polis, Jared	D
3	Tipton, Scott	R
4	Buck, Ken	R
5	Lamborn, Doug	R
6	Coffman, Mike	R

District	Name	Party
7	Perlmutter, Ed	D

Connecticut

District	Name	Party
1	Larson, John B.	D
2	Courtney, Joe	D
3	DeLauro, Rosa L.	D
4	Himes, Jim	D
5	Esty, Elizabeth	D

Delaware

District	Name	Party
At Large	Carney, John	D

District of Columbia

District	Name	Party
At Large	Norton, Eleanor Holmes	D

Florida

District	Name	Party
1	Miller, Jeff	R
2	Dunn, Neal	R
3	Yoho, Ted	R
4	Crenshaw, Ander	R
5	Brown, Corrine	D
6	DeSantis, Ron	R
7	Murphy, Stephanie *	D
8	Posey, Bill	R
9	Grayson, Alan	D
10	Demings, Val *	D
11	Nugent, Richard	R
12	Bilirakis, Gus M.	R
13	Christ, Charlie *	D
14	Castor, Kathy	D

District	Name	Party
15	Ross, Dennis	R
16	Buchanan, Vern	R
17	Rooney, Tom	R
18	Mast, Brian *	R
19	Clawson,Curt	R
20	Hastings, Alcee L.	D
21	Deutch, Ted	D
22	Frankel, Lois	D
23	Wasserman Schultz, Debbie	D
24	Wilson, Frederica	D
25	Diaz-Balart, Mario	R
26	Curbelo, Carlos	R
27	Ros-Lehtinen, Ileana	R

Georgia

District	Name	Party
1	Carter, Buddy	R
2	Bishop Jr., Sanford D.	D
3	Westmoreland, Lynn A.	R
4	Johnson, Henry C. "Hank" Jr.	D
5	Lewis, John	D
6	Price, Tom	R
7	Woodall, Robert	R
8	Scott, Austin	R
9	Collins, Doug	R
10	Hice, Jody	R
11	Loudermilk, Barry	R
12	Allen, Rick	R
13	Scott, David	D
14	Graves, Tom	R

Guam

District	Name	Party
At Large	Bordallo, Madeleine	D

Hawaii

District	Name	Party
1	Takai, Mark	D
2	Gabbard, Tulsi	D

Idaho

District	Name	Party
1	Labrador, Raul R.	R
2	Simpson, Mike	R

Illinois

District	Name	Party
1	Rush, Bobby L.	D
2	Kelly, Robin	D

District	Name	Party
3	Lipinski, Daniel	D
4	Gutierrez, Luis	D
5	Quigley, Mike	D
6	Roskam, Peter J.	R
7	Davis, Danny K.	D
8	Duckworth, Tammy	D
9	Schakowsky, Jan	D
10	Schneider, Brad	D
11	Foster, Bill	D
12	Bost, Mike	R
13	Davis, Rodney	R
14	Hultgren, Randy	R
15	Shimkus, John	R
16	Kinzinger, Adam	R

District	Name	Party
17	Bustos, Cheri	D
18	LaHood, Darin	R

Indiana

District	Name	Party
1	Visclosky, Peter	D
2	Walorski, Jackie	R
3	Stutzman, Marlin	R
4	Rokita, Todd	R
5	Brooks, Susan W.	R
6	Messer, Luke	R
7	Carson, André	D
8	Bucshon, Larry	R
9	Young, Todd	R

Iowa

District	Name	Party
1	Blum, Rod	R
2	Loebsack, David	D
3	Young, David	R
4	King, Steve	R

Kansas

District	Name	Party
1	Huelskamp, Tim	R
2	Jenkins, Lynn	R
3	Yoder, Kevin	R
4	Pompeo, Mike	R

Kentucky

District	Name	Party
1	Whitfield, Ed	R

District	Name	Party
2	Guthrie, S. Brett	R
3	Yarmuth, John A.	D
4	Massie, Thomas	R
5	Rogers, Harold	R
6	Barr, Andy	R

Louisiana

District	Name	Party
1	Scalise, Steve	R
2	Richmond, Cedric	D
3	Boustany Jr., Charles W.	R
4	Fleming, John	R
5	Abraham, Ralph	R
6	Graves, Garret	R

Maine

District	Name	Party
1	Pingree, Chellie	D
2	Poliquin, Bruce	R

Maryland

District	Name	Party
1	Harris, Andy	R
2	Ruppersberger, C. A. Dutch	D
3	Sarbanes, John P.	D
4	Edwards, Donna F.	D
5	Hoyer, Steny H.	D
6	Delaney, John	D
7	Cummings, Elijah	D
8	Van Hollen, Chris	D

Massachusetts

District	Name	Party

District	Name	Party
1	Neal, Richard E.	D
2	McGovern, James	D
3	Tsongas, Niki	D
4	Kennedy III, Joseph P.	D
5	Clark, Katherine	D
6	Moulton, Seth	D
7	Capuano, Michael E.	D
8	Lynch, Stephen F.	D
9	Keating, William	D

Michigan

District	Name	Party
1	Benishek, Dan	R
2	Huizenga, Bill	R
3	Amash, Justin	R

District	Name	Party
4	Moolenaar, John	R
5	Kildee, Daniel	D
6	Upton, Fred	R
7	Walberg, Tim	R
8	Bishop, Mike	R
9	Levin, Sander	D
10	Miller, Candice	R
11	Trott, Dave	R
12	Dingell, Debbie	D
13	Conyers Jr., John	D
14	Lawrence, Brenda	D

Minnesota

District	Name	Party
1	Walz, Timothy J.	D

District	Name	Party
2	Kline, John	R
3	Paulsen, Erik	R
4	McCollum, Betty	D
5	Ellison, Keith	D
6	Emmer, Tom	R
7	Peterson, Collin C.	D
8	Nolan, Rick	D

Mississippi

District	Name	Party
1	Kelly, Trent	R
2	Thompson, Bennie G.	D
3	Harper, Gregg	R
4	Palazzo, Steven	R

Missouri

District	Name	Party
1	Clay Jr., William "Lacy"	D
2	Wagner, Ann	R
3	Luetkemeyer, Blaine	R
4	Hartzler, Vicky	R
5	Cleaver, Emanuel	D
6	Graves, Sam	R
7	Long, Billy	R
8	Smith, Jason	R

Montana

District	Name	Party
At Large	Zinke, Ryan	R

Nebraska

District	Name	Party

District	Name	Party
1	Fortenberry, Jeff	R
2	Bacon, Don	D
3	Smith, Adrian	R

Nevada

District	Name	Party
1	Titus, Dina	D
2	Amodei, Mark	R
3	Rosen, Jacky *	D
4	Kihuen, Ruben*	D

New Hampshire

District	Name	Party
1	Shea-Porter, Carol	D
2	Kuster, Ann	D

New Jersey

District	Name	Party

District	Name	Party
1	Norcross, Donald	D
2	LoBiondo, Frank	R
3	MacArthur, Tom	R
4	Smith, Chris	R
5	Gottheimer, Josh *	D
6	Pallone Jr., Frank	D
7	Lance, Leonard	R
8	Sires, Albio	D
9	Pascrell Jr., Bill	D
10	Payne Jr., Donald	D
11	Frelinghuysen, Rodney	R
12	Watson Coleman, Bonnie	D

New Mexico

District	Name	Party

District	Name	Party
1	Lujan Grisham, Michelle	D
2	Pearce, Steve	R
3	Lujan, Ben R.	D

New York

District	Name	Party
1	Zeldin, Lee	R
2	King, Pete	R
3	Israel, Steve	D
4	Rice, Kathleen	D
5	Meeks, Gregory W.	D
6	Meng, Grace	D
7	Velázquez, Nydia M.	D
8	Jeffries, Hakeem	D

District	Name	Party
9	Clarke, Yvette D.	D
10	Nadler, Jerrold	D
11	Donovan, Daniel	R
12	Maloney, Carolyn	D
13	Rangel, Charles B.	D
14	Crowley, Joseph	D
15	Serrano, José E.	D
16	Engel, Eliot	D
17	Lowey, Nita	D
18	Maloney, Sean Patrick	D
19	Gibson, Chris	R
20	Tonko, Paul D.	D
21	Stefanik, Elise	R
22	Hanna, Richard	R

District	Name	Party
23	Reed, Tom	R
24	Katko, John	R
25	Slaughter, Louise	D
26	Higgins, Brian	D
27	Collins, Chris	R

North Carolina

District	Name	Party
1	Butterfield, G.K.	D
2	Ellmers, Renee	R
3	Jones, Walter B.	R
4	Price, David	D
5	Foxx, Virginia	R
6	Walker, Mark	R
7	Rouzer, David	R

District	Name	Party
8	Hudson, Richard	R
9	Pittenger, Robert	R
10	McHenry, Patrick T.	R
11	Meadows, Mark	R
12	Adams, Alma	D
13	Holding, George	R

North Dakota

District	Name	Party
At Large	Cramer, Kevin	R

Northern Mariana Islands

District	Name	Party
At Large	Sablan, Gregorio	D

Ohio

District	Name	Party
1	Chabot, Steve	R

District	Name	Party
2	Wenstrup, Brad	R
3	Beatty, Joyce	D
4	Jordan, Jim	R
5	Latta, Robert E.	R
6	Johnson, Bill	R
7	Gibbs, Bob	R
8	Boehner, John A.	R
9	Kaptur, Marcy	D
10	Turner, Michael	R
11	Fudge, Marcia L.	D
12	Tiberi, Pat	R
13	Ryan, Tim	D
14	Joyce, David	R
15	Stivers, Steve	R

District	Name	Party
16	Renacci, Jim	R

Oklahoma

District	Name	Party
1	Bridenstine, Jim	R
2	Mullin, Markwayne	R
3	Lucas, Frank	R
4	Cole, Tom	R
5	Russell, Steve	R

Oregon

District	Name	Party
1	Bonamici, Suzanne	D
2	Walden, Greg	R
3	Blumenauer, Earl	D
4	DeFazio, Peter	D

District	Name	Party
5	Schrader, Kurt	D

Pennsylvania

District	Name	Party
1	Brady, Robert	D
2	Fattah, Chaka	D
3	Kelly, Mike	R
4	Perry, Scott	R
5	Thompson, Glenn W.	R
6	Costello, Ryan	R
7	Meehan, Pat	R
8	Fitzpatrick, Michael G.	R
9	Shuster, Bill	R
10	Marino, Tom	R
11	Barletta, Lou	R

District	Name	Party
12	Rothfus, Keith	R
13	Boyle, Brendan	D
14	Doyle, Mike	D
15	Dent, Charles W.	R
16	Pitts, Joseph R.	R
17	Cartwright, Matthew	D
18	Murphy, Tim	R

Puerto Rico

District	Name	Party
At Large	Pierluisi, Pedro	D

Rhode Island

District	Name	Party
1	Cicilline, David	D
2	Langevin, Jim	D

South Carolina

District	Name	Party
1	Sanford, Mark	R
2	Wilson, Joe	R
3	Duncan, Jeff	R
4	Gowdy, Trey	R
5	Mulvaney, Mick	R
6	Clyburn, James E.	D
7	Rice, Tom	R

South Dakota

District	Name	Party
At Large	Noem, Kristi	R

Tennessee

District	Name	Party
1	Roe, Phil	R
2	Duncan Jr., John J.	R

District	Name	Party
3	Fleischmann, Chuck	R
4	DesJarlais, Scott	R
5	Cooper, Jim	D
6	Black, Diane	R
7	Blackburn, Marsha	R
8	Fincher, Stephen	R
9	Cohen, Steve	D

Texas

District	Name	Party
1	Gohmert, Louie	R
2	Poe, Ted	R
3	Johnson, Sam	R
4	Ratcliffe, John	R
5	Hensarling, Jeb	R

District	Name	Party
6	Barton, Joe	R
7	Culberson, John	R
8	Brady, Kevin	R
9	Green, Al	D
10	McCaul, Michael T.	R
11	Conaway, K. Michael	R
12	Granger, Kay	R
13	Thornberry, Mac	R
14	Weber, Randy	R
15	Hinojosa, Rubén	D
16	O'Rourke, Beto	D
17	Flores, Bill	R
18	Jackson Lee, Sheila	D
19	Neugebauer, Randy	R

District	Name	Party
20	Castro, Joaquin	D
21	Smith, Lamar	R
22	Olson, Pete	R
23	Hurd, Will	R
24	Marchant, Kenny	R
25	Williams, Roger	R
26	Burgess, Michael	R
27	Farenthold, Blake	R
28	Cuellar, Henry	D
29	Green, Gene	D
30	Johnson, Eddie Bernice	D
31	Carter, John	R
32	Sessions, Pete	R
33	Veasey, Marc	D

District	Name	Party
34	Vela, Filemon	D
35	Doggett, Lloyd	D
36	Babin, Brian	R

Utah

District	Name	Party
1	Bishop, Rob	R
2	Stewart, Chris	R
3	Chaffetz, Jason	R
4	Love, Mia	R

Vermont

District	Name	Party
At Large	Welch, Peter	D

Virgin Islands

District	Name	Party
At Large	Plaskett, Stacey	D

Virginia

District	Name	Party
1	Wittman, Robert J.	R
2	Rigell, Scott	R
3	Scott, Robert C.	D
4	McEachin, Don *	D
5	Hurt, Robert	R
6	Goodlatte, Bob	R
7	Brat, Dave	R
8	Beyer, Don	D
9	Griffith, Morgan	R
10	Comstock, Barbara	R
11	Connolly, Gerald E. "Gerry"	D

Washington

District	Name	Party

District	Name	Party
1	DelBene, Suzan	D
2	Larsen, Rick	D
3	Herrera Beutler, Jaime	R
4	Newhouse, Dan	R
5	McMorris Rodgers, Cathy	R
6	Kilmer, Derek	D
7	McDermott, Jim	D
8	Reichert, David G.	R
9	Smith, Adam	D
10	Heck, Denny	D

West Virginia

District	Name	Party
1	McKinley, David	R
2	Mooney, Alex	R

District	Name	Party
3	Jenkins, Evan	R

Wisconsin

District	Name	Party
1	Ryan, Paul D.	R
2	Pocan, Mark	D
3	Kind, Ron	D
4	Moore, Gwen	D
5	Sensenbrenner, F. James	R
6	Grothman, Glenn	R
7	Duffy, Sean P.	R
8	Ribble, Reid	R

Wyoming

District	Name	Party
At Large	Lummis, Cynthia M.	R

List of State Governors

Governors are subject to change. District of Columbia residents should answer that D.C. is not a state and does not have a capital. Residents of U.S. territories should name the capital of the territory.

Source: http://en.wikipedia.org/wiki/List_of_current_United_States_governors
January 2017

*Newly elected 2016 Subject to change upon Certification

Alabama Governor Robert Bentley

Alaska Governor Bill Walker

American Samoa Governor Lolo Matalasi Moliga

Arizona Governor Doug Ducey

Arkansas Governor Asa Hutchinson

California Governor Edmund G. Brown

Colorado Governor John Hickenlooper

Connecticut Governor Dan Malloy

Delaware Governor John Carney *

Florida Governor Rick Scott

Georgia Governor Nathan Deal

Guam Governor Eddie Baza Calvo

Hawaii Governor David Ige

Idaho Governor C. L. "Butch" Otter

Illinois Governor Bruce Rauner

Indiana Governor Eric Holcom *

Iowa Governor Terry E. Branstad

Kansas Governor Sam Brownback

Kentucky Governor Matt Bevin

Louisiana Governor Bobby Jindal

Maine Governor Paul LePage

Maryland Governor Larry Hogan

Massachusetts Governor Charlie Baker

Michigan Governor Rick Snyder

Minnesota Governor Mark Dayton

Mississippi Governor Phil Bryant

Missouri Governor Eric Gereltens *

Montana Governor Steve Bullock

Nebraska Governor Pete Ricketts

Nevada Governor Brian Sandoval

New Hampshire Governor Chris Sununu *

New Jersey Governor Christopher Christie

New Mexico Governor Susana Martinez

New York Governor Andrew Cuomo

North Carolina Governor Roy Cooper

North Dakota Governor Doug Burgum*

Northern Mariana Islands Governor Eloy Inos

Ohio Governor John Kasich

Oklahoma Governor Mary Fallin

Oregon Governor Kate Brown.

Pennsylvania Governor Tom Wolf

Puerto Rico Governor Alejandro Javier García Padilla

Rhode Island Governor Gina Raimondo

South Carolina Governor Nikki R. Haley

South Dakota Governor Dennis Daugaard

Tennessee Governor Bill Haslam

Texas Governor George Abbott

Utah Governor Gary Richard Herbert

Vermont Governor Phil Scott *

Virginia Governor Terry McAuliffe

Virgin Islands Governor Kenneth Mapp

Washington Governor Jay Inslee

West Virginia Governor Jim Justice *

Wisconsin Governor Scott Walker

Wyoming Governor Matthew Mead

List of State Capitols

Alabama - Montgomery

Alaska - Juneau

Arizona - Phoenix

Arkansas - Little Rock

California - Sacramento

Colorado - Denver

Connecticut - Hartford

Delaware - Dover

Florida - Tallahassee

Georgia - Atlanta

Hawaii - Honolulu

Idaho - Boise

Illinois - Springfield

Indiana - Indianapolis

Iowa - Des Moines

Kansas - Topeka

Kentucky - Frankfort

Louisiana - Baton Rouge

Maine - Augusta

Maryland - Annapolis

Massachusetts - Boston

Michigan - Lansing

Minnesota - St. Paul

Mississippi - Jackson

Missouri - Jefferson City

Montana - Helena

Nebraska - Lincoln

Nevada - Carson City

New Hampshire - Concord

New Jersey - Trenton

New Mexico - Santa Fe

New York - Albany

North Carolina - Raleigh

North Dakota - Bismarck

Ohio - Columbus

Oklahoma - Oklahoma City

Oregon - Salem

Pennsylvania - Harrisburg

Rhode Island - Providence

South Carolina - Columbia

South Dakota - Pierre

Tennessee - Nashville

Texas - Austin

Utah - Salt Lake City

Vermont - Montpelier

Virginia - Richmond

Washington - Olympia

West Virginia - Charleston

Wisconsin - Madison

Wyoming - Cheyenne

Avoid Scams / Evite las estafas de inmigración
From the USCIS website: http://www.uscis.gov/avoidscams

The wrong help can hurt

Are you getting the right immigration help?

Many people offer help with immigration services. Unfortunately, not all are authorized to do so. While many of these unauthorized practitioners mean well, all too many of them are out to rip you off. This is against the law and may be considered an immigration services scam.

If you need help filing an application or petition with USCIS, be sure to seek assistance from the right place, and from people that are authorized to help. Going to the wrong place can:

Delay your application or petition

Cost you unnecessary fees

Possibly lead to removal proceedings

This site can help you avoid immigration services scams. Remember: Know the facts when it comes to immigration assistance, because the Wrong Help Can Hurt.

Tools to Help You Avoid Scammers

USCIS wants to combat immigration services scams by equipping applicants, legal service providers and community-based organizations with the knowledge and tools they need to detect and protect themselves from dishonest practices.

To accomplish this goal, USCIS launched the Unauthorized Practice of Immigration Law (UPIL) Initiative. As part of the effort, we've partnered with several government agencies to identify resources that can help you avoid immigration services scams.

Empower yourself by using our online educational resources, which include:

The top things to know before and after filing an application or petition

A list of common immigration services scams

State-by-state information on where you can report an immigration services scam

Advice on finding authorized legal help

Information on becoming an authorized legal immigration service provider

Educational tools you can print and share

This page can be found at: http://www.uscis.gov/avoidscams.

Evite las estafas de inmigración

https://www.uscis.gov/es/eviteestafas

No queremos que usted se convierta en víctima de una estafa de inmigración. Si necesita ayuda legal sobre asuntos de inmigración, asegúrese de que la persona que le ayuda está autorizada a brindarle consejo legal. Solamente un abogado o un representante autorizado que trabaje para una organización reconocida por la Junta de Apelaciones de Inmigración (BIA, por sus siglas en inglés) puede darle consejo legal.

¿Quién puede ayudarle con sus preguntas de inmigración?

Si necesita ayuda con sus preguntas:

Llame al Centro de Servicio al Cliente de USCIS al 800-375-5283 (TDD, para sordos y personas con impedimentos auditivos : 800-767-1833)

Pregúntele a Emma (un asistente virtual que responde preguntas y le ayuda a navegar nuestro sitio web)

Encuentre ayuda legal autorizada

Verifique uno de nuestros próximos eventos de enlace o

Haga una cita en línea para visitar su Oficina Local de USCIS.

Herramientas para ayudarlo a protegerse de los estafadores

Combatimos las estafas de inmigración proveyéndoles conocimiento y herramientas a los solicitantes, proveedores de servicios legales y organizaciones de base comunitaria.

- Si usted recibe un mensaje de correo electrónico sospechoso, reenvíelo al buzón de USCIS Webmaster.

¿Ha sido testigo de alguna estafa de inmigración?

- Repórtelo a la Comisión Federal de Comercio (FTC, por sus siglas en inglés) llamando al 877-FTC-HELP, o puede presentar una queja en línea o

- Repórtelo a las autoridades locales o estatales.

Tome control utilizando los recursos educacionales en línea, que incluyen:

Las cosas más importantes que debe hacer antes de presentar una solicitud o petición

Una lista de las estafas de inmigración más comunes

Información por estado acerca de dónde puede reportar una estafa en los servicios de inmigración

Consejo sobre cómo encontrar ayuda legal autorizada

Información sobre cómo convertirse en un proveedor de servicios de inmigración autorizado

Recursos educativos que puede imprimir y compartir y

Ayuda y herramientas generales en línea.

ABOUT THE AUTHOR

Mike Swedenberg saw a need to assemble a study guide to help those persons wishing to immigrate to the United States whose second language is English. This study guide is annotated with the names of current Representatives that all applicants must know. The list is current for State Governors, US Senators and US Congressmen. This list will be updated at each election cycle.

Contact: Mike@Swedenberg.com

http://swedenberg.com

Other books by the Author

A New York Wedding – a novel

Bully Boss – a novel

The Road Warrior a sales manual

Advertising Copywriting and the Unique Selling Proposition

21 ½ Things to Know Before Self-Publishing a Book

Smart Money StupidMoney

How to Publish an eBook

CPSIA information can be obtained
at www.ICGtesting.com
Printed in the USA
LVOW13s1744221216
518443LV00007B/439/P